Alphabet You

.

Alphabet You

Love Messages

By

Gary Cleaton

First paperback edition 2022

ISBNs
Paperback: 978-1-80227-949-8
eBook: 978-1-80227-950-4

My dedication

With loss comes hurt and despair,
but in time there must also be healing.

I dedicate this book to the one who provides my inspiration,
and who put the meaning back into my life.

A is for adorable
N is for nice
D is for delightful
R is for radiant
E is for exquisite
A is for astonishing

Even her name spells out just how good she is.

Table of Contents

Preface

This book was written about feelings.
Never be afraid to express them.
Never be afraid to show them.
Never be afraid of them.
Love can be such an amazing thing,
so if you are ever lucky enough to be in love with somebody
tell them!
Otherwise, how else will they know?

A

A DATE

It starts by talking.
Plans are made.
Plans agreed.
The promise relaxes.
Anticipation mounts.
The day approaches.
The moment arrives.
The day is special.
The night divine.
You are a vision.
There is no equal.
You are my queen.
You are my world.
You are my love.
I have found you now.
And you have found me.
I'm staying always.
It's all I want to do.
I know you're worth it.
And I know your love is worth it.
I know my love is true.
And it's all just for you.

A FINE LINE

It's a fine line between want and need,
but ...
I don't need to hear you,
but I certainly want to.
I don't need to see you,
but I certainly want to.
I don't need to feel good,
but I certainly do when I'm with you.
I won't say I don't need you though,
because really I do,
And I certainly want you.

A GOOD THING

Don't worry just because one day
someone comes along and sees just how amazing you
really are.
And then thinks to himself "wow!"
You're everything I could ever wish for or want for the
rest of my life.
If you too think it's a good thing,
Be brave,
Take a chance.
It's just possible, likely even,
that it could be the best decision you will ever make.

A MIRACLE

A miracle is finding something impossible happen or come true.
My miracle was finding you and falling in love.
It has happened and it's true, and I'll be forever grateful to you.

A TOUCH

With that glint in your eyes,
I feel a touch of your love.
With the merest kiss from your lips,
I feel a touch of your love.
When we are cheek to cheek,
I feel a touch of your love.
With that smile on your face,
I feel a touch of your love.
With your hand in my hand,
I feel a touch of your love.
And all the times we are together,
I feel the touch of your love.
Just because you can't say it,
doesn't mean I can't feel it.

ALL IT TOOK

All it took was just one look.

Hypnotised by your eyes,
spellbound by your stare,
totally lost in the blue,
that is everything that is you.

Captured in the depth,
I learnt to dance.
I never really had a chance.

Totally smitten, total dedication,
I have finally found my life's salvation.

ALONE

When I'm alone all is not lost,
I sit at my computer and turn to Microsoft.
Words come easy as my fingers scurry
and as the lines extend I tend not to worry.
This forced lockdown and separation
cannot destroy our strong foundation.
I picture you and the places we've been,
our trips to the services to fill with caffeine.
There's no moments lost or ever forgotten,
I only wish they were more often.
Not a single time we've ever hung out,
will I ever be able to forget about.
One thing for sure that I don't doubt,
I love you so very much day in and day out.

ALPHABET YOU

You are

Amazing, Astonishing,
Beautiful, Bright,
Caring, Classy, Considerate,
Divine, Dependable, Desirable,
Elegant, Electrifying,
Fabulous, Funny,
Generous, Gorgeous,
Helpful, Honest,
Illustrious, Intelligent, Inspirational,
Joyful, Kind, Loving,
Marvellous, Nice, Opulent,
Pleasant, Playful, Quaint,
Radiant, Respectful, Rare,
Sophisticated, Sensual, Sweet,
Thrilling, Unselfish,
Valued, Wonderful, Yummy.

I could go on forever but truthfully, none of these words can really do you justice.

AMAZED

I am amazed by your beauty
and by your soul.
I am amazed by your kindness
and by your actions.
I am amazed when I listen to you
and by what you say.
I am amazed by your courage
and by your commitment.
I am amazed by you
and I love you.

B

BAD DAYS

When you are having a bad day,
I will sit with my arms around you.
When your soul is troubled,
I will sit still and listen.
When you are feeling happy,
I will rejoice in your smile.
When you need attention,
I will lavish it upon you.
When you seek solitude,
I will keep a safe eye from a distance.
Whenever or whatever,
I will be your everything.
Because that's what you are to me.
My everything.

BECAUSE OF YOU

Because of you, I don't just see the sky.
I now notice the different patterns that the clouds make.
I see the countless birds as they fly in front of the blue backdrop.
It's with awe that I notice the bright sun slowly rise and again as it sets.

Because of you, I don't just exist.
I now marvel at the feeling of being part of something unique and special.
I thrive on the excitement of all the new things that we do.
I cherish the thought of being together for a long time.

Because of you, I don't just exist.
Colours now seem so much more vibrant.
Flavours stand out more on my taste buds.
My emotions swell my heart with pride till I feel it will burst.

Because of you, I don't just exist.
I live.

BELIEVE

I believe in you,
and everything you do.
I believe in all that you are,
and all that you will be.
I believe in your sense of right,
and in your judgment.
I believe in your actions
and in your commitment.
I believe in our relationship,
and the path it's on.
Why?
Because I believe in us.

BLESSING

You are everything I could ever want,
everything I could ever dream of,
more than I could ever hope for,
and the most amazing blessing possible.
You are just you,
but you are unique,
and I love you so much.

C

CAN I?

Can I touch you?
Can I hold you?
Can I love you?

When you're with me I look and admire.
When I dream of you I imagine.

Can I touch you?
Can I hold you?
Can I love you?

When we are out I'm filled with pride.
When we are in I'm full of thanks.

Can I touch you?
Can I hold you?
Can I love you?

When you're away I remember fondly.
When you're at a distance I want you closer.

Can I touch you?
Can I hold you?
Can I love you?

When I talk of you it's with pride.
When I speak about you it's with feeling.

Can I hold you?
Can I touch you?
Can I love you?

When I make plans they are for you.
When I look to the future it's you.

Can I hold you?
Can I touch you?
Can I love you?

CAN'T FORGET

I can't forget,
I won't forget,
I couldn't forget.
The things that you do,
The way that you are,
The way that you make me feel.
My love for you is constant,
My love for you is real.

CANNOT BELIEVE

Can't believe how my heart has grown.
Can't believe how it has not blown.
My feelings just keep getting stronger.
And I know I'll feel them forever or longer.
You have brought the light back to this boy,
when I am with you what's not to enjoy?
My life is full of merriment and humour,
and I can only see you in my future.
If you choose to see it through,
I'll spend my whole life loving you.

CATCH 22

It's a catch 22.
I want to tell you how much I love you,
and just how much I care about you,
how much I desire you
and how much I cherish you.
But I worry that saying it so much
may water down the meaning behind it,
and I wouldn't want that at all.
On the other hand, you deserve to be told,
you should be told.
You deserve to be reminded.
You also deserve all my effort and attention.
And that my dear,
is the catch 22.

CHANGED

You've changed me,
and without a shadow of a doubt,
most certainly for the better.
I see things differently now,
much more clearly.
I feel things more intensely now,
much more deeply.
I feel free to express my feelings,
I also feel the need to do so.
I have an urge for experiences and adventures,
just so long as they include you.
I'm happy with the man I am now,
and I'm happy with my choices.
I'm happy with you.

CHANGED OUTLOOK

You have changed me,
and you have changed my goals.
I now have a new outlook on life,
one with a meaningful future ahead.
Some things do not matter to me anymore,
some things mean more,
although nothing means more than you do.
I feel alive, I feel hope, I feel a purpose,
but mostly I feel a belonging.
I belong with you,
I love you.

COLOURS

You bring so much colour into my life.
Yellow, because you are like the sunlight.
Green, because you bring new life to me.
Red, because you make my blood pump so fast.
Gold, because you make my life so rich.
Pink, because you're such a lady and so feminine.
Blue, is totally washed away when I'm with you.
Black, because you make me notice the moon.
White, because of my thoughts of togetherness.

CONNECTION

The very real connection we have
can never be broken or ignored,
can never be walked away from,
and will certainly never die.
If you're so connected with each other,
as I feel we are,
the connection will remain intact
despite time and distance,
or any other circumstance.
Real connections live on forever.
So will we.

CONSTANT

You are constantly on my mind,
and always in my heart.
My actions are governed by my thoughts of you,
and my deeds will always place you first.
You have brought real meaning back into my life,
and it's now set firmly in the right direction.
Walk by my side with me,
and together we can show everyone
just what a real love story should look like.

COULD OR WILL

No one could love you more.
No one will love you for longer.
No one could love you better.
No one will work as hard.
No one could try as much.
No one will want it more.
No one ever could.
No one ever will.

D

DAYS OUT

A day out with you is a day to be seized.
I'm so at ease and delightfully pleased.
It's a day to be cherished,
and a day to be remembered,
a lifelong memory to be kept and treasured.
Experiences can never be measured,
no limit should ever be put on our pleasures.
So I'll take all the opportunities that fall to me,
as a life with you is just so full and lovely.

DESIRE

My desire for pleasure,
and my desire for feeling good,
are both inspired by
my desire for you.

DESIRE THAT OVERFLOWS

You need to know just what an effect you have had on me.
My heart overflows with desire for you.
I'm filled right to the brim with happiness.
My pride when I'm seen with you is immeasurable.
And my love has no boundaries.
I will not imagine my life without you.
There is no life without you.
Always and forever
I will love you.

DREAMS OF US

I lay in bed and dream of us,
it's a great dream to have and always a plus.
I dream of travels and adventures to come,
of Cape Verde and others all in the sun.
No riches or baubles could ever replace,
nothing is more valuable than your embrace.
With you by my side nothing more would I need,
for I am in love and that I concede.
So I look to the future with happiness in mind,
the two of us together always aligned.
Love has me bitten, love holds me tight,
nothing could fill me with more delight.
I love you now I'll love you forever,
do I doubt myself,
no not ever.

E

EASY

It's so easy to say I love you,
and so easy to fall in love.
But don't take the words lightly,
I mean everything above.
You light up my life,
and bring a joy to my heart.
Such an amazing lady,
from whom I never want to part.
You bring me such pleasure,
and excitement too,
I could never love anyone more than I love you.

ENOUGH

There are no flowers bright enough
to give to you.
There's no song written good enough
to sing to you.
There's no praise worthy enough
to offer to you.
There's no destination good enough
to take you to.
There will never be enough
time to spend with you.
There could never be enough
words to explain my love for you.

ENOUGH TIME

I could never spend enough time with you.
Whenever I leave your side, I wish I was back with you.
You're fun, entertaining, great company,
and just amazing to look at.
However,
there is one thing that has changed
over the years that I have known you.
It's simply I have grown to
love you more and more.
I am happy, content, privileged
and honoured to be able to call you my partner,
and I will stand by your side
lovingly
for the rest of my life,
if you'll let me.

EVERLASTING

You are not one in a million,
there is no one else quite like you on the planet -
there never could be.
In you I see everything I like and everything I adore.
You're more than I deserve and more than I could ever
hope for.
I'm so thankful I get the chance to prove to you
what we have is real and everlasting.
Love you.

EXCHANGE

Love has brightened the darkest of my days.
Love has mended all of my ills.
Love has brought new meaning to my life.
Love has given me great hope for the future.
You can exchange the word love
for your name,
and it would mean the same.
Thank you my love.

EYES

Through my eyes I see you.
Through my eyes I see hope.
Through my eyes I see joy.
Through my eyes I see excitement.
Through my eyes I see happiness.
Through my eyes I see safety.
Through my eyes I see compatibility.
Through my eyes I see love.
Through my eyes I see a future.

EYES WIDE OPEN

I didn't just fall in love with you,
I walked in with my eyes wide open.
I see only beauty before me,
I see only caring and kindness.
I welcome the feelings you gift to me,
I cherish you just the way you are.
I know my love is true,
I feel it deep in my heart.
I want it to last forever,
I believe it will.

F

FEELINGS

I can't run, I won't run.
I can't hide, and I won't hide.
I can't control them, but then I don't try to anyway.
These feelings that I have for you are quite simply amazing.
Whenever I am with you, I feel like I have known you
forever.
I feel comfortable, relaxed and happy. I can be myself.
I love nothing better than putting a smile on your face,
and there are no ends I wouldn't go to, to achieve just that.
I'm so lucky to have met you, and so glad that you have
given us both
the chance to build a friendship into the relationship
that we now have,
boyfriend and girlfriend.
What a great feeling.

FIND OR FOUND

They say love isn't something that you find,
but something that finds you.
Well whatever is right,
I have definitely found love,
or love has definitely found me.
Either way,
I know I'm madly in love with you.

FLOWER

You've stayed as tight as a bud
for as long as you need to.
It's now time for you to bloom again,
and show off the beautiful flower
that I can see and know that you are.

FLOWERS

I would pick flowers for you every single day,
and I would play music for you right away.
I would sit and listen to you speak,
and I would watch over you as you fall asleep.
I would protect you with my life,
even though we are not yet man and wife.
I would give you everything I possibly could,
don't let me ever be misunderstood.
I will forever fight in your corner,
and always be your number one supporter.
Our love means everything to me,
that I freely give, promise, and guarantee.
I only have one more endeavour,
and it comes with no added pressure,
It's just to make sure that hopefully,
we will stay together.

FLOWERS FOR YOU

These flowers are for you
because you care about others,
because you think of others,
because you worry about others,
because you are there for others,
because you do so much for others.

These flowers are for you
because I care about you,
because I think of you,
because I am there for you,
because I love you.

FOR YOU

What would I do for you?

I would climb a hill for you.
Well, there aren't any mountains around here.

I would walk over hot coals for you.
Well, I'd have to leave my shoes on.

I would wrestle a bull for you.
Well, at least a calf.

I would make you smile endlessly.
Well, I already act the fool so I am halfway there.

I would make love to you all night.
Well, who wouldn't want to.

I would love you forever.
Well, I have no choice in that,
As I am already hooked.

FOREVER

I will gaze at you forever.
I will stay with you forever.
I will want you forever.
I will admire you forever.
I will cherish you forever.
I will desire you forever.
I will be proud of you forever.
I will love you forever.

FRIENDSHIP

Our friendship was the best possible
way to start this love story.
I'll always remember the days we spent as friends.
But I'll always hold closer the days that I have
spent in love with you.

FUTURE

We have so much to live for.
So many more special days ahead.
We can plan together.
It will last forever.
This love will keep us alive.
This love is strong.
This love is here to stay.

G

GENUINE

The feelings I have for you are very real and genuine,
and that also includes caring for you very deeply too.
They are clear in my mind, as are my hopes and wishes.
I genuinely hope we can be happy together forever.
I don't foresee any reason why we shouldn't be.
Have courage, take a breath
and take a chance on me.
I promise you won't regret it.

GET ME

You just get me.
You understand my moods my feelings,
my quirks and my wishes.
Your willingness to engage, accept
and even nurture my weaknesses
show not only the strength of your character,
but also your commitment to this relationship.
You can't always make the right decisions in life,
but if your heart can just get one right,
then a lifetime of happiness can follow.
I trust in my heart,
I trust in you.
I'm now looking forward to that lifetime of happiness.

GREATEST FEELING

There is no greater feeling than
being in love and being loved in return.
Everything seems so right and so real;
a natural belonging along with a sense of purpose.
It makes life's journey a joy to travel.
Shared delights double the reward
as it calms the chaos of life,
and brings real meaning to each new day.
Loving you is both a privilege and rewarding.
I am yours forever.

H

HAPPINESS

Happiness is when I hear your voice.
Happiness is when I get to see you.
Happiness is when you smile at me.
Happiness is when I wake up and you're beside me.
Happiness is what you give to me.
All I want is to do the same for you.

HAPPY WHEN

I'm happy when
I get to wrap my arms around you,
and feel your heart pounding in your chest.

I'm happy when
I have your head rested on my shoulder,
so I can feel your soft hair against my cheek.

I'm happy when
the intensity of my blood coursing round,
is matched by the speed of your own.

I'm happy when
I get to look upon you longingly,
only to see the same look reflected in
your very own eyes.

I'm happy when
I declare my love for you with no doubts,
and for you to accept and to love me back too.

HOLD

You give me your hand to hold,
I give you my heart in return.
I will always hang on to your hand,
I want you to always hang on to my heart.
I will keep you safe in my hand.
Will you keep my heart safe in yours?

HOLDING

You hold....
a beauty so abundant,
a nature so sweet,
a kindness so inspiring,
a soul so worthy,
a belief so resolute,
a laughter so infectious,
a love so desirable,
and my heart in your hands.

HONOURED

A sweet and charming lady,
you wear the prettiest of smiles upon that face of yours.
You only ever seem to allow the brightness to show through,
with no hint or clue of any hidden past darkness or turmoil.
I know you have gained a strength and an independence,
taught to you by yourself because of lessons you have
had to learn.
It's a strength that you do not use against others,
but one that you only strive to protect yourself with.
I see all this clearly, and it is the very least that should be
expected.
Because of all this I find myself
honoured to know you,
honoured to spend time with you,
honoured to be your boyfriend,
and honoured to be in love with you.
You are among the rarest of people,
you are very, very special.

HOPE

Love can find us all,
and so it should.
It sometimes comes when it's least expected.
But love is so worth it and should be welcomed.
Sometimes the journey to it
can be longer than expected,
but it's so worth the wait,
as the reward can be so great.
I am deeply in love with you.
And I hope with all my heart,
that you,
fall deeply in love with me too.

HOPE AND DREAMS

We have a love that is worth risking everything for.
A future that is worth hoping for and dreaming about.
The dream itself holds no fear for me,
but failure scares the hell out of me.
I could not now imagine my life without you in it.
You are not just part of my life,
you are my life.
Your happiness is my happiness,
your dreams are my goals,
and your smile is the warmth in my heart.
I give to you all my love for always.

HOROSCOPE

Life is great,
life is good,
even if it's not all quite understood.

Why am I blessed?
Why am I lucky?
I have only gone and found my hunny,

The future looks bright,
the future holds hope.
Was this seen in my horoscope?

I will treat you right,
I will do you no wrong,
for I'm not trying to string you along.

You are my soulmate,
my partner too.
There's nothing we cannot sail right through.

And so you don't ever doubt or misconstrue,
I have to tell you now that after review,
fear not girl,
I'll always love you.

HOT

Your eyes melt me.
Your lips are delectable.
Your face is beautiful.
Your body is divine.
Your skin so soft.
Your hair so fine.
No wonder I think you're so hot.

I

I AM

Undoubtedly I am an intense person with deep feelings.
I constantly use my heart as well as my mind to think
things through.
I have a sensitive soul, luckily,
still relatively untouched by many troubles.
I also have some innocence left that shouldn't really
belong to me at my age.
This all adds up to make me the man that I am.
I believe I am:
trusting and trustworthy,
dependant and dependable,
wishing to be loved and wanting to love.
My heart/mind and soul are all in unison.
My conclusion,
I have a yearning for you,
my all-consuming thoughts want you to be my fellow
soul-mate.
I love you deeply and want to walk the long path with
you by my side.

I AM NOT

I'm not afraid to express my love to you.
It's pure and honest and I give it freely.
You should hear that.
I owe it to you and myself to be true.
I hope it gives you similar feelings to the ones that I feel
when I am with you,
or even just thinking about you.
It's a special feeling that comes from deep within my
heart and warms my soul.
I am not afraid to love you always.

I CAN'T

I can't see you enough,
think about you enough,
or be with you enough.
I don't know what you have done to me,
but I'm gloriously happy about it.
I will worship you always.
I will want you always.
I will love you always.

I COULD

I could never stop loving you.
I could never walk away.
I know our love is real.
I know we can make this work.
I could never imagine it not.
I wouldn't want to.
This love is real.

I DON'T DO LOCKDOWNS

I don't enjoy this separation,
I know that's not a revelation.
I don't enjoy this incarceration,
I know this isn't any vacation.
I don't enjoy this deprivation,
I know this is more than an irritation.
I don't enjoy the frustration,
I know I have to wait for the cessation.
I don't enjoy waiting for the cancellation,
but I know I will then have the elation.

I DON'T HAVE

I don't have to try to love you,
I do.
I don't have to try to hold on to you,
I don't have to try to treat you,
I do.
I don't have to try to inspire you,
I don't have to try to respect you,
I do.
I don't have to try to listen to you,
I don't have to try to admire you,
I do.
I don't have to try to please you,
I don't have to try to commit to you,
I have.

I HAVE

I have …
No interest in a life on my own.
No interest in growing old on my own.
No interest whatsoever in other women.
No interest in causing any heartache.
No interest in false declarations.
No interest at all in a life without you.

But I do have an interest …
A deep interest to share my life with you.
An interest to discover new pleasures with you.
An interest to commit fully to you.
An interest to please, satisfy, and nurture a relationship
with you.
An interest in giving and receiving endless love with you.

I JUST CAN'T

I can't keep my eyes off of you,
I can't keep my hands off of you,
I can't keep you out of my dreams,
I can't imagine a life without you,
I can't keep away from you,
I can't help the way I am,
I can't stop adoring you,
I can't believe my good fortune,
I can't help loving you.

I LOOK AT YOU

I look at you
and my breath is taken from me.
I look at you
and it's hard to breathe.
I look at you
and I'm tongue-tied.
I look at you
and I just can't stop talking.
I look at you
and I'm blinded.
I look at you
and I see your beauty.
I look at you
and I don't have a care in the world.
I look at you
and I know I care about you.
I look at you
and I want nothing more.
I look at you
and I want you.
I look at you
and I think about my future.
I look at you
and you are my future.

I LOVE

I love the connection.
I love the commitment.
I love the excitement.
I love the intimacy.
I love the sincerity of it all.
I love the sense of belonging.
I love the rarity of what we have.
I love the happiness I am feeling.
I love the inspiration you stir up.
I love the thought of where this is going.
I love the thought of you.

I MEAN IT

I believe it and I mean it:
all the things I have said,
all the things I have done,
prove to me you are the one.

I believe it and I mean it:
the way that I feel,
the way that I act,
prove to me you are the one.

I believe it and I mean it:
the pain of missing you,
the pain of separation,
prove to me you are the one.

I believe it and I mean it:
the wish to hold,
the wish to kiss,
prove to me you are the one.

I believe it and I mean it:
this can't be undone,
don't want just anyone.
It proves to me you are the one.

I believe it and I mean it.

I NEED

I need you happy.
I need you joyous.
I need you smiling.
I need you content.
I need you excited.
I need you fulfilled.
I need you pleased.
I need you peaceful.
I need you gratified.
I need you in my life.
I need you.
I want you.
I love you.

I THINK OF YOU BECAUSE

I love your soft touch.
I love your eyes looking at me.
I love to feel your hot breath.
I love to kiss your lips.
I love the softness of your skin.
I love your body next to mine.
I love your arms wrapped around me.
I love the smell of your hair.
I love your innocence.
I love your naughtiness.
I love the way you make me feel.
I just love thinking about you.

I WANT

I want you to be happy.
As I am. Blissfully.
I want you content.
As I am. Fully.
I want you excited.
As I am. Thankfully.
I want you to be in love.
As I am. Completely.
I want you to want us.
As I do. Hopefully.
I want you to want it forever.
As I do. With all my heart.

I WANT TO BE

I want to be the man that tells you every night
that he loves you.
Then I want to be the man that spends every day
trying to prove it to you.
I'll also be the man that says he'll always be there,
then I'll hang around forever to prove I'm no liar.
You are everything, always, and in every way,
the one I want to be with.

I WANT YOU

I want you to be my inspiration.
I want you to be my motivation.
I want you to be my stimulation.
I want you to be my influence.
I want you to be my incentive.
I want you to be my hope.
I want you to be my joy.
I want you to be my reality.
I want you to be my love.
I want you to be my pride.
I want you to be my desire.
I want you to be my ecstasy.
I want you to be my delight.
I want you to be my soulmate.
Oh wait, you already are.
I just want you to want me.

I WANT YOU TO FEEL

I want you to feel like never before.
I want you to feel incomparable romance.
I want you to feel you have found the right one.
I want you to feel safe and trust in our journey.
I want you to feel gloriously happy.
I want you to feel completely content.
I want you to feel so very loved.
I want you …

I WAS

I was broken, now I'm mended.
I was hurt, now I'm healed.
I was sad, now I'm happy.
I was lost, now I'm found.
I was alone, now I'm not.
I was down, now I'm high.
You are my saviour.

I WILL

I will love you each day come what may.
I will love you each evening with my whole being.
I will love you each morning as it's so warming.
I will love you each week I'm on a winning streak.
I will love you each month there's never enough.
I will love you each year without any fear.
I will love you for a lifetime not just sometime.

IF EVER

If ever you feel yourself doubting
just how far you can go,
remember how far you have come.
Remember everything you have faced,
all the battles you have won,
all the fears you have overcome.
You are right by the finishing line now.
You have made it.
Never-ending happiness awaits you.
I await you.

IF I WANT

If I want to see some beautiful eyes,
I can look into yours.
If I want to gaze at a beautiful face,
I can look at yours.
If I want to see inside a beautiful soul,
I can look into yours.
If I want to see perfection,
I just have to look at you.
If I want to see my heart's desire,
I just have to look at you.
If I want to see my future,
I just have to look at you.
There's really no "ifs" about it,
when I look at you.

IF LOVE IS

If love is a blessing, than I've been blessed.
If love is a feeling, then I've been touched.
If love is an attraction, then I'm attracted.
If love is a sport, then I am game.
If love is caring, then I care.
If love is pride, then my chest will swell.
If love is happiness, then I can only smile.
If love is eternal, then I'll love you forever.
If love is you, then I'm in love.

IF YOU WERE

If you were a flower,
you would have the prettiest look.
If you were a dessert,
you would have the sweetest taste.
If you were a painting,
you would be nothing short of a masterpiece.
If you were a star,
you would undoubtedly be the brightest.
If you were my girlfriend,
you would be the best.
No ifs,
you are.

INSTRUMENT

When I met you
I felt a chord firmly struck in my heart.
Now the sweetest melodies constantly play in my head.
I can feel the rhythm of my heart,
just like you hear the beat from a drum.
I could quite easily dance for the rest of my life now.
You have hit all the right notes.
You are the instrument of my happiness.

IT IS REAL

I always tell you how I feel,
and that's because to me it's real.
I stand by everything I have said,
I just can't get you out of my head.
I'm so in love with you,
it will always be forever true.
Please give me a chance to show I care,
for I know you can be the answer to my prayer.
I see everything I want and everything I need,
together our life will be good, guaranteed.
But it's not all about me as we are a team,
so let's stick together and live life like a dream.

IT'S NOT

It's not lust, it's passion.
It's not admiration, it's pride.
It's not satisfactory, it's bliss.
It's not attraction, it's captivation.
It's not good looks, it's beautiful.
It's not wonderful, it's magical.
It's not a crush, it's a relationship.
It's not for a while, it's for life.
It's not like, it's love.
It's not me, it's us.

L

LIFE

My eyes are open wide to the world.
But it's only you that I see.
Blood rushes around my body.
But it's you that pumps my heart.
It's air that lets me breathe.
But it's you that makes me live.

LIFETIME

If we had a lifetime
I would spend it gazing at you.
If we had a lifetime
I would spend it listening to you.
If we had a lifetime
I would spend it caring about you.
If we had a lifetime
I would spend it loving you.
If we had a lifetime
I would wish to spend it all with you.

LOCKDOWN 1

We haven't held hands for ages.
We haven't kissed for an age.
We haven't hugged forever.
We haven't had some pleasure.
I really don't like us being apart,
but you still, and will,
always hold my heart.

LOCKDOWN 2

I can't see you,
but I can feel you.
I can't see you,
but I can dream of you.
I can't see you,
but I can still want you.
I can't see you,
but I can talk with you.
I can't see you,
but I can and do sure miss you.
Despite this setback
I will always love you.

LOOK AT YOU

When I look at you
I see your natural beauty,
I see your caring attitude,
I see your empathy,
I see you're so likeable,
I see your attractive personality,
I see your intelligence,
I see your courage,
I see your thoughtfulness,
I see your love,
I see my future.

LOVE IS

Love is
wanting to share
and wanting to care.

Love is
wanting to live
and wanting to give.

Love is
wanting to nourish
and wanting to cherish.

Love is
wanting to stay
wanting to always.

Love is
wanting to pursue
and wanting to be true.

Love is
wanting to pleasure
and wanting to be together.

Love is you.

LOVE SO REAL

With love so real
time flies so fast.
With love so real
I'd like it to last.
With love so real
it feels so vast.
With love so real
it dwarfs the past.
With love so real
it's a different class.
With love so real
it's easy to forecast.
With love so real
I stand steadfast.

M

MAKE

I want to make you happy,
I need to make you happy,
I will make you happy.

I want to make you smile,
I need to make you smile,
I will make you smile.

I want to stay with you,
I need to stay with you,
I will stay with you.

I want to love you,
I need to love you,
I do love you.

MY LADY

You are a lady,
a very special lady.
You are the lady of my dreams,
my very special dreams.
You are the lady in my future,
a very special future.
You are the lady I love,
a very special love.

MY LIFE

You are by far the best thing that's happened to me.
You have shown me that the darkness can be pushed aside.
You have come along and shown me the fantastic
pleasures to be found.
I now have a renewed impetus to make the most out of
the rest of my life.
My life with you.

MY LOVE

My love for you is deep and has no limits.
It is totally unconditional and given freely.
I promise it will remain unchanged forever,
as it comes from an endless supply,
replenished daily from my overflowing heart.
There will never need to be a time when
you doubt me,
as every day I will remind you,
just how very special you are to me.

MY LOVED ONE

Here I am laying in my bed,
with nothing but thoughts of you
running through my head.
As they turn to dreams later,
of my love it will be a true indicator.
I have nothing to hide and no need to lie.
You my darling have put a twinkle in my eye.
Your beautiful looks and kindly nature,
no one could have more or have any greater.
My yearning for your company has no limits,
but there never seem to be enough minutes.
The precious times that we do share,
make me feel like I'm a millionaire.
My love has grown to such a height,
and the life I now live is such a delight.
The one thing that I honestly got right,
was listening to my heart when it had the foresight.
You are amazing and you are sweet,
when you're not around I feel incomplete.
You make me happy and you make me whole,
you have taken me over heart and soul.
We still have so many things to do,
as all before has been a preview.
This fantastic journey of ours has begun,
and I couldn't be happier.
You are my loved one.

MY PATHS

I don't regret this path I have chosen to follow.
From my thoughts and imaginations of the future
I can see only good times ahead.
You have shed light on my hidden dreams and given me
hope that they will come true.
No other person could possibly gel with me the way you
have.
We have an understanding for each other that is so
special and probably unique.
You are my hopes, my wishes and my dreams,
and I love you so much.

MY PROMISE

My promise to you ...
To want you forever.
To protect you forever.
To never let any harm come to you ever.
To help you in any way I can forever.
To always be there for you forever.
To make you smile forever.
To hug you forever.
To kiss you forever.
To care for you forever.
To be with you forever.
To love you forever.

N

NIGHTS

We've now spent a handful of nights together,
to start with we were just lounging around purely at our
leisure.
While I note there's no capacity big enough to measure,
I do still try to find such words to express my pleasure.
Undoubtedly you will always be my number one
treasure,
and despite my constantly high blood pressure,
All I ever hope for is,
it is forever.

NO SURPRISE

It's not surprising I love you.
You are beautiful,
you are cute,
and you are so very sexy.
Then I find you funny, exciting and adventurous.
Also your intelligence and knowledge,
make you interesting.
Not to mention you are the best of company.
Never stood a chance, did I?

NO ONE CAN

No one but you can ...
make me so happy,
bring me such joy,
lift my spirits up high,
fill me with anticipation,
excite me so much,
give me immense strength,
dominate my dreams completely,
ever mean more to me.

NOT

I'm not the best looking guy you could attract.
I'm not the slimmest guy you could attract.
I'm not the youngest guy you could attract.
I'm not the richest guy you could attract.
I'm not the fittest guy you could attract.
But
No other guy could adore you more.
No other guy could respect you more.
No other guy could be inspired more.
No other guy could be smitten more.
And,
despite the millions of men out there,
no one could love you more.

NOT HARD

It's not hard for me to be loyal to you,
it's something I couldn't ever imagine not being.
It's not hard for me to love you either,
it's not something I couldn't imagine not doing.
It's certainly not hard being around you,
it's not something I could ever imagine not wanting.
It's not hard with you as part of my life,
it's not something I could imagine without you.
It's not a hard life at all,
it's a fantastic life with you.

NOT SCARED

I'm not scared to love you.
I'm not scared to show my feelings for you.
I'm not scared to show my affection.
I'm not scared to stand by you.
I'm not scared to stand up for you.
I'm not scared to dedicate my life to you.
But as you mean so much to me,
and have turned my life into a beautiful thing,
I am scared of losing you.

O

OFTEN AS I CAN

I like to look at you as often as I can.
I do find it so hard to keep my eyes off you.
I see such a beautiful woman before me,
and I can't help but admire you.
You do something special to my inner body,
It's a feeling I find impossible to explain,
but it sure is a feeling that I like.
With you willing to share your precious time with me,
I realise just how so damned lucky I am.
My promise to you,
is to always strive to be worthy of you.

ONCE UPON A TIME

Once upon a time I met a girl.
She certainly had the looks to attract my attention.
Then I found out she had a beautiful personality too.
I grew fonder and closer until I was hooked.
Now I can't imagine my life without her.
Why would I ever want to?
She makes me happy, she makes me complete.
And I want to be able to do the same for her.
I will be there for her in her hour of need.
I will always be there for her for anything.
In my life dreams can come true.
I'm looking for a happy ever after with this girl.
That girl is you.

ONE IN A MILLION

You are different.
There is something so very special about you.
You're the one star to shine out brightly
in amongst a sky of a million others.
They go completely unnoticed,
but you don't.
My heart is yours forever.
It's safe with you.
I know you'll protect it,
for you're that one in a million.
My one in a million.

P

PASSION

You've reawakened and relit a passion in me.
It now burns much brighter and more intense than I
have ever felt before.
It is an eternal passion that will never be able to be
quenched or extinguished.
It is all completely pointed towards you,
for you, and for nobody else,
ever.

PLEASE

From out of the darkness,
you have lit up my life so brightly.
I will never be able to fully repay you,
but I will try for the rest of my life.
Your smile has cast a spell to last.
Forever I am yours,
Will you please be mine?

PROMISE

I promise to you as our relationship continues to blossom,
that I will nurture it and never neglect it.
You are wanted and will never be taken for granted.
I will always treat you with respect,
and never show any kind of contempt.
I will always be completely honest,
and never be devious or untruthful.
I will always be kind, and never cruel.
I will always be there for you,
I will never be unreliable.
For as long as you want me,
I will want you.

Q

QUESTION

Do I love you?
With all my heart.
When did I love you?
Almost immediately.
Why do I love you?
Because you're perfect.
How do I love you?
With a passion.
Will I always love you?
Undoubtedly.
Is the love worth it?
Unquestionably.

R

REASONS

You are my reason ...
For being happy.
For being hopeful.
For being grateful.
For being thrilled.
For being delighted.
For being satisfied.
For being brave.
For being who I am.
For being in love.

REMEMBER ALWAYS

You are a wonderful and beautiful woman.
You are wise, intuitive, intelligent and funny.
You have friends that care deeply about you,
and you have others that deeply love you.
This is because they all know you are worthy.
Don't ever doubt yourself;
from what I've learned from you,
there isn't anything you couldn't accomplish if you tried.
I feel truly blessed to know you,
and I want the very best of everything for you.
You continue to brighten my life daily,
And I will always strive to do the same for you.

REFLECTION

With time to reflect,
and time to consider,
I sit alone just after my dinner.

My thoughts are of one,
and my wishes too.
All I want is to be with you.

As the days tick by,
and the nights follow along,
these special feelings can't be wrong.

You captured my eye,
and you won my heart.
I'll let nothing tear us apart.

My love is strong,
my love is true.
And all of it belongs to you.

I'll try to stay brave,
and I'll try to stay strong,
by thinking of you all day long.

I miss you so much,
and I miss you so badly.
I just want to see you, oh so madly.

I'm sorry I put us both through this,
and I'm sorry that I went away.
Believe me I have regretted it every day.

But I'll soon be back,
and by your side.
I bet neither of us stays dry-eyed.

I love you so much,
and I love you so dearly,
I've never said anything quite so sincerely.

REMINDER

It's my wish to always remind you every day,
just how much I love you.
If you ever have a doubt, please tell me.
then I will double my efforts until you are sure again.
I can't let you ever believe that this isn't forever.
It can be, it should be, it will be, it is.
You mean the world to me.
You are my world.

S

SHADES OF BLUE

Faded and jaded, and looking quite tainted,
there are many different shades of blue,
when I'm not around you.
But it all turns around once you've been found.
Life again flows and mellows,
as blues cross back over to yellows.
Colours are enhanced, enriched and brightened
as all my feelings heighten and again lighten.
Everything is back to normal, back to peace,
as once again I am reunited with my masterpiece.
You!

SHORT AND SWEET

It may be short,
it may be sweet,
but time with you cannot be beat.

You may be far,
you may be near,
but you always bring such great cheer.

You may be cautious,
you may bide your time,
but I have no doubt that we'll be fine.

You may now relax,
you may learn to trust,
I know it will take time for you to adjust.

I may have wrecked,
I may have altered,
your chosen path that has been halted.

Your plans have gone but please look forward,
I think I'm what your doctor ordered.

The dreams you had,
the path you'd take,
now takes two to participate.
I'm with you all the way.

SMILING

I do not kid or fool,
I want to make sure our lives are fun.
My soul is singing,
and my heart is pounding,
I don't have a minute to lose.
I want to show you the world,
and shower you with love.
I want to make sure I constantly
spread a smile across your face.
Whether it be from pleasure,
laughter or awe, I don't mind.
Your smile is intrinsically linked to my own happiness.
I now dedicate the rest of my life
to see you smiling.

SO LUCKY

I'm so glad I met you
I feel so lucky.
You call me your partner
I feel so lucky.
I meet your friends
I feel so lucky.
We do such nice things together
I feel so lucky.
We make plans ahead
I feel so lucky.
I wake up next to you
I feel so lucky.
You care deeply about me
I feel so lucky.
I love you
I am lucky.

SOMETHING ABOUT YOU

There's just something about you,
it could be your blue eyes.
There's just something about you,
it could be your pretty face.
There's just something about you,
it could be your infectious laugh.
There's just something about you,
it could be your amazing body.
There's just something about you,
it could be your caring nature.
There's just something about you,
but whatever it is,
it's you that I love.

SOMETHING SPECIAL

When you only think about one other person,
and when you only want the very best for them.
When there never seems enough time,
and what there is disappears so quickly.
When you are both apart,
but still feel linked.
When you are totally at ease together,
and never need pretend.
When you hang on to every word,
but also simply listen to their voice.
When your heart races,
and a wide smile comes so easy.
You should hang on to each other,
You've found something special.

SOPPY

Sometimes I just feel so soppy.
We have had some great conversations.
All were enlightening and absorbing.
But I can never stop telling you,
how much I love you,
how much I care about you,
how much you mean to me.
I'm totally smitten, totally happy, and totally yours.
I wouldn't change a thing
and I'm eagerly awaiting all that's to come.
You are an adorable and amazing lover,
the best of company, and a great friend,
all in one.

SORRY

I'm sorry, but I care so much.
I'm sorry, but I adore you.
I'm sorry, but I find you so attractive.
I'm sorry, but I want to be with you.
I'm sorry, but you are the only one for me.
I'm sorry, but I'm not going anywhere.
But I'm certainly not sorry I love you.

SOUL

You have a truly amazing soul.
I would have to be blind not to see it.
I would have to be crazy not to recognise it.
I would have to be mad not to appreciate it.
I would have to be foolish not to help nurture it.
I would have to be stupid not to relish it.
I would have to be mindless not to admire it.
And I would have to be utterly insane,
not to love you for it.

SPIRIT

You have so much spirit and strength,
you're such a strong and independent lady.
It doesn't scare me at all though.
It's part of you now,
and I fell in love with you as you are.
I know you can stand your ground if you need to,
should the occasion ever arise.
But I will always be there for that little extra helping
hand when, and if, it's ever needed.
I will be the rock you can depend on forever.

SPORT

If being in love was a sport …
I'd score the winning goal.
If being in love was a sport …
I'd be top of the league.
If being in love was a sport …
I'd be the world champion.
If being in love was a sport …
I would be a winner.
Being in love must be a sport …
I've already won the greatest prize

STRONG LOVE

I have the strongest love known,
with a heightened passion
deeply entwined with unbridled enthusiasm,
and an intense fervour for romance with you.

A fondness with no equal,
an emotional appetite running equal
and parallel alongside a lustful sexual desire,
not solely due to your immense magnetic attraction,
but from my overwhelming and undying love for
perfection personified.
You.

SUCH JOY

Just a fleeting moment,
such joy it brings to me.
To see you in person,
such joy it brings to me.
To hold and wrap you in my arms,
such joy it brings to me.
To sit and listen, sometimes in awe,
such joy it brings to me.
To know you care so deeply,
such joy it brings to me.
The things we do the places we go,
such joy it brings to me.
To think of the future, happy I believe,
such joy it brings to me.
I love you.
such joy it brings to me.

T

TEARS

Over the years
I've cried many a tear
some through hurt
some through fear.
All my tears are now from joy.
Sheer joy and happiness
gifted to me by you,
accepted with gratitude and respect.
All to be returned four-fold.

THAT ONE PERSON

When that one person
lifts you up,
when that one person
makes you smile,
when that one person
guards your back,
when that one person
doesn't mind your idiosyncrasies,
when that one person
often puts you before themselves,
that one person is your soul mate.
That one person is you.

THE ONE

The one who thru pride can increase my height.
The one that makes things seem so bright.
The one that helps make everything right.
The one I think of holding my pillow tight.
The one I dream of every night.
The one who with no effort can excite.
The one I'll never give up on without a fight.
The one that brings me such delight.
And the one I love with all my might.

THE REASON

You are the reason my heart beats so fast
and the reason that my heart skips a beat.
You are the reason I freely gave my heart away
and the reason that my heart is full of hope.
You are the reason my heart and soul are united
and the reason my heart feels so blessed.
You are the reason my heart is grateful
and the reason my heart is so thankful.
You are the reason I surrendered my heart
and the reason my heart is so full of love.

THEY

They keep me going.
They warm my heart.
They increase my heart rate.
They make me proud.
They inspire me.
They are a source of encouragement.
They turn me on.
They are sweet memories.
They mean everything.
And they certainly make me smile.
That's what every picture I have of you
means to me.

THRILL ME

You thrill me when you just stand close to me.
You thrill me every time you reach for my hand.
You thrill me to my core when you look in my eyes.
You thrill me with your soft sensuous touches.
You thrill me with your words of encouragement.
You thrill me with a passion for our future.
You thrill me with the bond that we are building.
You just damn well thrill me.

TIME

Time is an enemy.
I have always hated the clock ticking down,
ready to put a temporary stop to our happiness.
I feel cheated out of precious moments with you,
when finally the hands have stretched as far as they
possibly can for the occasion.
Pulling apart and saying goodbye will always leave me
with a tinge of sadness,
however magical all the moments before have just been.
Because time without you,
Is just lost time with you.

TO SEE YOU

I love to see you smile.
I love to hear you laugh.
I love to feel your touch.
I love to touch you.
I love your eyes.
I love the look in your eyes.
I love your beauty.
I love you in my dreams.
I love your cuteness.
I love how you make me happy.
I love your kisses.
And I love you because you're you.

TO TOUCH

To touch you is my wish.
Because....
to touch you is so sweet,
to touch you is so divine,
to touch you is so exciting,
to touch you is so rewarding,
to touch you means so much,
to touch you is a privilege,
to touch you means I am with you.

U

UNDERHAND

I love you so
and always try to let you know.
You still find it hard to understand
but my honesty I promise, is not underhand.
The way you make me feel is real,
I'm more alive than I deserve to feel.
It's all thanks to you and your precious time,
your thoughts and actions stick in my mind.
How can I ever repay you in kind?

UNWELL

I have an illness.
When I think about you I can't concentrate on anything.
When I'm with you it's hard not to just stand and shake uncontrollably.
One minute I can be in a cold sweat,
the next a hot flush.
I think I'm going blind too, as I can see nothing except you.
My illness is love,
and I absolutely love it.

UPDATE

A relationship update,
just so you know …
I still enjoy your company immensely.
I still love all the things that we do together.
I still want to be around you all the time.
I'm still always thinking about you.
I still think you're amazingly beautiful.
I still think you're kind and caring.
I still think you're incredibly sexy.
I'm still grateful to have met you.
I'm still madly in love with you.
I'm still gloriously happy.
I'm still hoping for a future with you.

V

VERY VERY FAST

Racing along like a ship with tall masts,
so very very fast.
Striving to arrive and not to be last,
so very very fast.
Ever quicker and having a blast,
so very very fast.
My life before me now, hiding my past,
so very very fast.
The change in me never to be surpassed,
so very very fast.
Transformed and recast,
so very very fast
The love I carry so complete and so vast,
still so very very fast.

VIBRANT

My life is full of hope and excitement,
so full of colours bright and vibrant.
With hearts and soul together in alignment,
as we visit places and meet with friends.
The joy that I feel and the love I receive,
means there's nothing I can't attain or achieve.
Planning for the future, no doubts in my mind,
we'll walk together with our hands entwined.
Embracing each day, we can face it all,
as I feel so proud while walking tall.
Commitment and honour, respect too,
there isn't anything we couldn't get through.
So I dedicate my life and my love too,
And I promise this easily, as it's for you.

W

WAITING

I will always keep on loving you,
albeit for a while, from a distance.
Although it won't be easy,
nothing will dampen my resolve,
and I know my heart is strong enough to see me
through.
To me this isn't a test,
it's merely just a hurdle,
and I'll manage to get over it somehow.
For the prize isn't glory,
it's you waiting on the other side,
with your hugs and kisses,
your sparkling eyes,
your warm embrace,
and your softest of touches.
All this means it will be worth the wait,
however hard.

WET WITH WINE

I love your lips when wet with wine,
but only when they're joined with mine.
It's not just the wine that I taste,
it's love's desire so full of my haste.
I feel my full passion flowing,
as I sense my skin is glowing.
Our souls unite and join so tight,
I could never fight it despite my might.

And later together as we sleep tight,
I will dream of your lips tasting of wine,
of course still joined together with mine.

WHAT IT MEANS

Your lips on mine, and what it means.
A wanting so deep with feelings so intense.
Satisfaction is guaranteed as delight abounds.
Emotions run amok
and heart rate quickens.
A pleasure with no equal,
a joy to behold.
As proud as punch,
a bee with the honey.
No single thing as great,
as nothing could compare.
My hopes for the future easy to explain,
would simply be,
more of the same.

WHAT JOB ARE YOU?

You are a musician,
with a divine instrument,
playing the melody of my soul;
your music softly sounding in my ears.

You are an artist.
with a magical brush;
painting the picture that I wish to see,
your colours dancing in front of my eyes.

You are a doctor,
with a kind bedside manner;
taking away all of my ills,
making my heart beat stronger and fast.

You are a teacher,
impressing with your knowledge,
enthralling me with your intelligence,
teaching me lessons I wish to know.

There isn't anything you couldn't do.
You are all and everything to me.

WHEN

When I found you,
I also found
a partner in crime,
a trustworthy confidant,
a lifetime companion,
an amazing lover,
a true friend,
a soulmate,
my equal,
my future.

WHEN I CAN'T SEE YOU

When I can't see you
I think about you.
When I think about you
I write about you.
When I write about you
I visualise you.
When I visualise you
I imagine you.
When I imagine you
I think of the future.
When I think of the future
I dream.
When I dream it's of you.
Life just seems so wonderful.

WHEN YOU THINK

When you think your life's over
know that it's not.
When you think things can't improve
know that they will.
When you can only see the darkness
trust in the light.
When you are down in the dumps
don't dare despair.
Be hopeful and optimistic,
confident and positive.
Life is good.
Life is great.
You've proved that to me.

WHERE I WANT TO BE

Whenever I'm around you
I'm at ease,
I'm inspired,
I'm content,
I'm enthralled,
I'm ecstatic,
I'm satisfied,
I'm proud,
I'm peaceful,
I'm happy,
I'm grateful.
I'm where I want to be.

WITH YOU

With you as my lover I couldn't be happier.
You as a lover could never be matched.
As my lover there could never be another.
As a lover you take me to a high.
As a lover, you certainly leave me dry.
As my lover you make me feel complete.
As my lover no one else will ever compete.

WORDS

There are literally hundreds of words that I could use to describe
what I see when I look at you ...
Beautiful, stunning, gorgeous, amazing, attractive,
lovely, pretty, cute, elegant, ravishing, glamorous,
charming, delightful, irresistible, exquisite, magnificent,
flawless, radiant.
On and on the list goes.
Then there's the list of how I feel when I'm actually with
you ...
Joyful, proud, ecstatic, content, delighted, blessed,
exhilarated, excited, jubilant, delirious, blissful,
thankful, fortunate and lucky.
You're everything in every way to me
and I will love you forever.

WORSHIP

I worship the way you talk
and the way you walk.
I worship your eyes
and your glorious thighs.
I worship your lips
right down to your fingertips.
I worship your hair
whenever I'm there.
I worship your love
for it will always be enough.

WORTH

Your worth is much more than any diamonds or gold
could ever bring.
You're worth every early morning or late night to catch a
sunrise or sunset together.
You are worth much more than just second thoughts,
you are always my first thoughts.
You're worth all my time, all my effort and all my
commitment.
You are worth a lifetime of happiness.
You are more than worthy of my love.

Y

YOU

You are the reason I write
You are the reason I smile
You are the reason I'm happy
You are the reason my heart skips
You are the reason I get excited
You are the reason I look forward
You are the reason the word amazing exists
You are the reason I am in love.

YOU (ALWAYS)

Who's on my brain?
YOU!
Who's in my thoughts?
YOU!
Who commands my dreams?
YOU!
Who do I care about?
YOU!
Who do I wish to see?
YOU!
Who do I wish to hold?
YOU!
Who makes me happy?
YOU!
Who holds my heart?
YOU!
Who do I adore?
YOU!
Who is my soulmate?
YOU!
Who do I love?
YOU! YOU! YOU!

YOU ARE THE ONE

You are the one,
we have so much fun.
You are the one,
your looks can stun.
You are the one,
you bring out the sun.
You are the one,
a perfect companion.
You are the one,
the brightest beacon.
You are the one,
the one in a million,
the one I love.

YOU HAVE

You have brought such a huge amount of light into my life.
It has helped push my darkness far back into a deep recess.
My emptiness once feeling so great,
has been replaced by a fullness that I feel in my now
mended heart,
helping it beat true and strong again.
I can, and do, smile all the time, and my sleep pattern
has returned.
More often than not this brings fond and exciting
dreams of you.
I couldn't be happier with my life right now.
I couldn't be happier with you right now.

YOU MAKE ME

You make me see,
you make me feel,
you make everything real.

You make me laugh,
you make me smile,
you make everything worthwhile.

You make me strong,
you make me believe,
you make me never want to leave.

You make me whole,
you make me complete,
you make me land on both feet.

You make me live,
you make me alive.
Because of you,
now I can thrive.

.

Printed in Great Britain
by Amazon